WHEN A BAND-AID
IS NOT ENOUGH

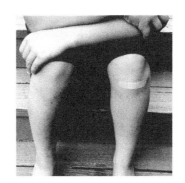

When A Band-Aid Is Not Enough

Identifiers:
ISBN-13: 978-1536811933
ISBN-10: 1536811939

ISBN: 9781311370976 (ebook: Smashwords.com)

First edition July 2016

10 9 8 7 6 5 4 3 2 1

Photos courtesy of the author.

This is a work of non-fiction. All the events are true,
but the names have been changed to protect privacy.

WHEN A BAND-AID IS NOT ENOUGH

A Mother's Harrowing Journey
Through Her Sons' Addiction to Prescription Drugs

PAM BASIL

DEDICATION

There are many people to thank for their support. This book is for:

MY PARENTS, who taught me the value of life, love, and family. Their gift has made me the person I am today.

MY FAMILY AND FRIENDS, whose unconditional love has guided me and given me hope, especially when all seemed hopeless.

MY SONS, who are my life. They have filled my life with joy, tears, and laughter. I am so blessed to call them my sons. I love their "hearts of gold" forever.

MY GRANDCHILDREN, who will always have my heart; may they never know the devastating effects of addiction in their lives.

ALL PARENTS, who may benefit from the words of hope this book offers. *When a Band-Aid is not Enough* is written from my heart. As I recorded the events and heartaches of dealing with my sons' addictions, I was strengthened and reinforced by my career as a social worker in which I have been blessed serving individuals with developmental disabilities. I admire their amazing hearts and perseverance. My whole life, both personally and professionally, has been dedicated to helping others... especially my sons, and through this journey, I have learned the difference between helping and enabling. There is always hope. *When a Band-Aid Is Not Enough* is my first book.

Chapters

Blake and his dirt bike

1. A Mother's Heartbreak

It is a beautiful sunny afternoon in the spring of 2007. I am sitting in the back yard feeling the warmth of the sunshine on my back after foot surgery last week brought my daily routine to a screeching halt. I have been able to do pretty much nothing. Living in the moment is foreign to me. So I am taking advantage of this downtime to step into the journey of documenting our family history.

I have spent most of my adult life coming to terms with my birth mother leaving me at the age of three. A family was not what she wanted in life at that time. Ironically, my mother and I lived in the same town until she moved out of state when I was in my forties. On the day before she left, I stood in her driveway saying goodbye again. Only this time, I wasn't three years old, although I cried like a child. Where did all those tears come from?

From a young age, I have been caring for others. I am the oldest of four daughters. While growing up, my parents called me "little mother hen." I was supposed to be the responsible one and guide my sisters. Then I was a single parent for seventeen years, nurturing and protecting my boys. I have also worked in a helping profession for forty years serving the developmentally disabled population. And today, just for today, on this lovely springtime day in the backyard, I have to take care of myself and recuperate. Do I even know how? Surely, somebody out there needs me! I can hobble on crutches to someone's aid!

As a woman in her "middle years," I have experienced many joys and heartaches. Two of my biggest joys were the births of my sons. Two of my deepest heartaches have been the chemical addictions of my sons. When I was blessed with children, I made myself a promise that I would never abandon them; I would always be involved. I would be there to place Band-Aids on boo-boos and wipe away tears.

When my boys were four and six years old, their father and I divorced. Then I felt I had to be both parents. I was scared and worried about failing them. I went to every game, went through boxes of Band-Aids, and dried tears. At times, we laughed until we cried. My sons were never going to feel I wasn't there for them. They were not going to feel the loss of a mother's love. Never in a million years could I have imagined that the disease of addiction would take over the lives of two of my loved ones. Not only that, I discovered that the effect of addiction on family members is just as devastating as the effect on the addict.

I have spent hours, days, and years attempting to answer the questions: When? How? Why? Why? Why? I have spent hours, days, and years trying to fix it. There were days when I just went through the motions of daily routine. My mind and heart were consumed with trying to save my boys' lives. How could I live my life when this addiction had the capacity to kill my sons? My oldest son often chided me that I was trying to put a Band-Aid over a bleeding artery. But addiction was not a boo-boo I could put a Band-Aid over and kiss the hurt away.

There were many times through the years that I blamed myself as a mother. If only I did this, didn't do that, said this, or didn't say that. I had no personal experience with drugs and addiction, so why did my sons? Was there something I could have, should have done? Short of placing them in plastic bubbles, I did the best I knew how. That's it! The best I knew how. Was it perfect? Flaw-proof? Certainly not, but I do know that everything I did or said was out of love.

The minutes, weeks, and years of my life that I spent trying to cope and control my sons' addictions were monumental. Looking back, I have learned new ways to deal with it. I did the best I knew how. Al-Anon puts it so well: "You didn't cause, it, you can't control it, and you can't cure it." (Al-Anon support groups provide important information and help for family members of addicted persons.)

I KNOW there were times God was guiding me. I know, because I had no clue what steps to take next. But sometimes a message would come in the middle of the night. I would awaken from a bad dream or have a new idea. I know now that God was leading me. I know God saved my boys and me. He was with us in those times of desperation and feelings of endless fear and hopelessness. On the days I could "Let Go and Let God" (Al-Anon), I found some serenity in a grandchild's hug,

a playful dog and a beautiful sunset. And some days that was…
well enough.

2. The Beginning of the Journey

Where and how did it all begin? I have asked myself that question countless times and through countless speculations. Was it a result of the divorce? A single mother raising sons? Peer pressure? Dealing with life losses? Back injuries or prescription pain pills?

My youngest, Blake, has been both headstrong and a dreamer since he was a little boy. He loved sports, and he was talented. He enjoyed the outdoors and lived to take risks. He especially liked anything with a motor attached. At the age of eight, Blake just had to have a scooter, then he just had to have a motor attached to it. We asked every man we knew if a motor could be attached, to no avail. Blake hoped for a miracle.

Then there was the dirt bike. I remember so clearly meeting with a father selling the bike of a son who had outgrown it. I really couldn't afford the $300 asking price, but I had never seen Blake's eyes light up so much as when we paid the $300 and took the bike home. That bike was the catalyst for so many laughs and happy memories, not to mention the scraped up bodies for both of my sons.

Did Blake's addiction begin at age 16?

What a turbulent year that was. He had gotten in with the wrong crowd. One of the most horrific times was the week that Blake ran away. He was tired of school, pushing his brother and me further away, and most likely began to experiment with pot. I could not go through the motions, as I was beyond worried about him. I could not work, sleep, or stop crying. When he returned home, we tried to get back to some sort of normalcy, but honestly, the innocence of my little boy was gone from his eyes...forever. My young son, only sixteen himself, also became a father that year. I now look at those pictures taken when his child, my grandson Brady, was a baby and see the young face of Blake.

During Blake's eighteenth year, his cousin and best friend died in a horrible accident. The pain and heartache overwhelmed us all. Looking back, it is now obvious that Blake did not deal with this loss. He masked his feelings and numbed himself with pain pills prescribed for a back injury.

During the same time, my oldest son, Mike, was involved in a work related accident that resulted in prescription pain pills for a back injury. At one time, both of my sons were in two separate rehabilitations.

Through it all, I tried to be the best parent possible to my sons. In my own childhood, I received conflicting messages, but thank goodness for my father and stepmother, who gave me the love and encouragement that was sadly missing in my relation-ship with my birth mother.

3. My Parents

I have spent most of my life trying to figure out how a mother can leave a child—how my mother could leave me at the age of three. Most of my early memories are of my father. Thank God for my dad.

My parents met in St. Augustine, Florida, when my dad was stationed in Jacksonville. He was quite the handsome Navy fellow and he fell head over heels for Theresa. It was not long until they were married and within nine months I was born. Nineteen months later, my sister Cassie arrived.

I have few memories of my mother when I was young. The ones I do recall would not warm a child's heart. I do not remember any nurturing—what a child yearns for and needs most. I do recall feeling protective of my sister, Cassie. While the details are sketchy, I vividly remember comforting Cassie in a bedroom, all by ourselves. Early on, our bond was cemented in our hearts.

In most cases of divorce in the 1950s, the mother was awarded custody of the children. My dad hung on to the last hope that he could "take my little girls home." At the custody hearing, he got his wish. My mother never bothered to show up. Cassie and I were going home with daddy!

After the divorce, my sister and I stayed with our aunt and other family members when our father was working. He was an over-the-road truck driver and could be gone for several days at a time. I would cry myself to sleep at night, scared to death my daddy wasn't coming back for us. I closed my eyes tight and prayed that he would come back for my sister and me. After all, our mother did not come for us…maybe daddy would leave us too. "Don't worry, Cassie. I will take care of you," I tried to reassure my little sister.

Thankfully, my father always returned. I felt safe with him. Even in the midst of turmoil, I felt reassured deep in my heart that he would always take care of us. And he did. He worked hard and he always came home to his girls. He played softball with us, he taught us how to swim, and he made us laugh, but he wasn't real savvy with "girly things." One morning while getting us ready for church, he used Brylcreem (a hair gel popular in the sixties that was thick as engine oil) on our hair. "A little dab will do ya" was the slogan, but he figured our long hair needed more than a little dab. We went to church looking like slicked-back rats, and it took a week to wash the gunk out of our hair.

Within a couple of years, dad met the woman I have called "mom" all my life. When they started to date, Cassie and I did not come up in conversation for a while. When my dad started to fall in love with her he was nervous about saying, "Oh by the way, I have two little daughters." She was shocked to learn about this ready-made family but came to know us and love us.

Shortly after that, they were married and we became a family!

Within a couple of years, sister number three came along and two years later, sister number four was born. We were a family of six, and with five females in the house, my dad did not stand a chance. Certainly, we had our troubled times, financial crises, and sibling rivalry, but we had each other. We had hope.

We took a vacation every summer, usually to the ocean, where my love of the water came to be one of my passions. I could spend hours sitting on the beach watching the waves and pondering the vastness of the ocean. I felt a sense of calmness and peace like nowhere else.

I had the security of family. We shared Sunday evenings making "Chef Boyardee" pizzas and watching our favorite television, the "Ed Sullivan Show." My mom made breakfast for us before school each morning, and we all sat down together at the dinner table every night. Our summers were filled with bike riding and roller-skating in the neighborhood. My sisters and I, along with neighborhood friends, would put on talent shows for our parents. (We all were aspiring Hollywood performers.) On Halloween, we would walk in groups through the neighborhood, filling our pillowcase sacks sometimes two or three times. On Thanksgiving, we had no idea how much we had to be grateful for. We were just living and loving our lives together.

Christmas time was the best. I have a fond memory of my Greek Grandpa staying overnight on Christmas Eve with our family. He was there to "protect" the gifts under the tree. Cassie and I woke up and tiptoed down the hall in the wee hours, but as soon as we reached the living room, Grandpa let out the loudest snore we ever heard. Needless to say, it worked and we retreated as fast as our legs would carry us.

My sister and I did not see much of Theresa, our biological mother, when we were growing up, even though she lived just across town. Sometimes, she would make plans to visit and then not show up. My dad said I would wait by the window waiting and watching for a mother who often did not come. How heartbroken I was to give up hope when the day ended. But the times we did spend with her do not evoke pleasant memories. I remember a couple of Sunday afternoon visits with her and her husband, when my sister and I were probably eight and ten years old. Riding in the back seat of their car on our way to dinner with them, we were not allowed to touch anything, nor make a sound, nor even say anything. To do any of these would upset her husband, and Theresa did not want to put him in a bad mood. At the house we couldn't touch anything either. We were made to sit on a white couch with our hands folded in our laps. At their dinner table, there was no excitement, no talking, laughing, or spilling milk. We never found out what would have happened if we broke any of their rules, but the anticipated fear was overwhelming.

Sometimes on the ride back my sister and I would get the giggles; maybe it was the thought of going home. Her husband would "tsk, tsk," and Theresa would quickly admonish us to "behave back there." Behave? We had been on our best behavior for the past three hours. Arriving home, Cassie and I would dash from the car and flee to our front door. We were home—yes, our loving home, thank God. But when I would go to bed those nights, I remember feeling sad too. Even though I didn't really know my mom, I missed her. That little girl missed her mother. What was she really like? Did she love us even a little bit? Sometimes, I would cry myself to sleep.

It appeared Theresa was comfortable with her choice of a different life, one where children did not fit in. My dad, bless his heart of gold, is not like her, and I feel so blessed that he shaped my heart. Well into my adult life, I resented Theresa. I struggled wondering why she didn't want Cassie and me and why she even had us. As fate would have it, I grew up to look like Theresa, which I did not welcome. It angered me when my aunts and grandparents would remind me that I look just like my mother.

When I became a parent, I attempted to have a heart to heart talk with Theresa. I wanted to ask her how she could leave us. Did she have any regrets? But she was heartbreakingly cold, aloof, and unemotional. Her only answer was, "You were better off with your dad." What? Yes, I know that, but tell me about YOU…you as a mom, your feelings, your hopes, your dreams and wishes. I wished for so many years that a door would open. I was hoping that I could get to know this woman who gave me life. But thirty years later, that is still the only answer I have: "You were better off with your dad."

4. Wedding Bells

Taylor and I were high school sweethearts. I fell in love with his sense of humor. Besides my dad, Taylor was the only one who could make me laugh until my sides ached. When we were still dating four years after high school graduation, my exasperated father asked us if we were planning to date for the rest of our lives. With that little nudge, we decided to get married. Taylor was the son my parents never had, and the big brother to my sisters. We all loved him.

For the first six years of our marriage, we shared a little apartment, worked during the week, and socialized with our friends on the weekends. Life was good. Then I learned the joyous news that I was pregnant. It remains one of the happiest moments of my life. My first child! It felt like I was the one and only pregnant woman in the world. I took care of myself, and my husband took care of me. Being pregnant was one of the best experiences of my life. Taylor and I attended natural childbirth classes. I was going to do this right all the way through.

One Saturday about two weeks from my due date, Taylor and I had spent nearly the whole day shopping for baby things. It was a great day. At home later, I started hemorrhaging. "I don't think this is normal," I said to Taylor, who frantically called the doctor. "Get to the ER immediately," the doctor ordered. I was feeling no pain except for the knot in my stomach fearing for my life while Taylor drove seventy miles per hour toward the hospital. He took "immediately" seriously.

Upon arrival, I was whisked to the ER in a wheelchair. Everything was happening so fast: blood pressure cuff on my arm, thermometer in my mouth, and needle sticks in my arms. In a flash, I was on a surgery table, being prepped for a C-section delivery. I asked Taylor to call my sister, who lived about ten minutes away. Taylor met her at the surgery entrance just long enough to give her his watch and say, "This is an emergency, and we could possibly lose both of them." Then he quickly shut the door, leaving her in a panic and wondering if we would ever see each other again. Thank God, in about an hour I had a beautiful baby boy. Mom and son were just fine. So were dad and aunt.

I felt a great sense of protectiveness toward my son, Mike. Maybe it was enhanced by the clenching fear of losing him during childbirth. I just wanted to do everything right, and I wanted him to be all right. For a first time mother, it would be great if babies were born with a "how to" book in their hand. I know I would have felt more confident with that information. But I do know that becoming a mommy in the winter of that year was the highlight of my life. Mike seemed to change daily during his first couple of years. I loved watching him grow and the way he made me laugh. He loved his Transformers and matchbox cars. He was a special little boy with a heart of gold—kind and thoughtful beyond his years.

My happiness doubled with the birth of our second son, Blake, two years later. But along with the joy came the unwelcome realization that Taylor and I were growing apart. He was gone from home a lot. We stopped communicating. Priorities changed and trust was broken. We continued through many trials and tribulations, but after years of growing up together and after twelve years of marriage, the fateful day arrived. The dissolution of our marriage that mid-October day in 1987 will forever be etched in my broken heart. My whole life changed. From that day forward, I was a single parent.

At ages six and four, Mike and Blake endured the heartache of divorced parents. There was plenty of disappointment, resentment, and, tears. My heart ached for my sons. They were feeling the fears of abandonment, just as I had as a child. This was the last thing I ever wanted for them. I felt such feelings of failure. Why did this happen?

Looking back, I can see that Taylor suffered the effects of growing up with alcoholism in his own family that might have helped cause the difficulties between us. Our interests and focuses were not on the marriage, and we grew further apart as alcohol became an outlet for Taylor. I knew very little about the ramifications of growing up with alcohol abuse, but Taylor did. I thought he hated everything about alcohol, and I felt sure he wouldn't want any part of it for himself or his family. Taylor seldom drank at home, and as far as I knew, was not drinking away from home either. In retrospect, I closed my eyes to the growing trouble. Had I opened them and acknowledged he was in the grips of alcoholism, I could have opened a channel of communication. We possibly could have tackled our difficulties together, instead of going in opposite directions.

I had lost hope.

Mike at Disneyworld

5. Single Parenting

After the dissolution the boys and I started on a roller coaster ride that took us on some welcomed highs, but to the lowest lows as well. Mike, at his tender young age, appointed himself the family protector. No one was going to hurt his brother or mother. And he extended this feeling to others. He was the one who gave his allowance to the homeless man on the corner or picked up the stray puppy. His heart of gold just continued to get bigger.

With each passing birthday, my boys grew taller and more independent. We created memories that made us cry and some that made us laugh until we cried. We carried on our summer vacation tradition. Collectively, the three of us would choose a destination for our summer vacation. On the road trips, inevitably, the boys would ask, "Mom, are we lost?" and I always had to answer, "Yes." Eventually, we would get there and have the time of our lives.

One summer, when the boys were still young, we flew to Disney World along with a hermit crab that Mike had won in a Parks and Recreation program the week before. Believing that animals belonged in their natural habitat, I thought it best to take him back to the shore. I carried the little creature in a cardboard box while trying to manage my sons and the luggage, even holding the box on my lap on the plane.

Upon arrival, the first thing the boys wanted to do was head for the hotel pool. So away we went, leaving the hermit crab safe in its cardboard box in the rental car. I really didn't consider the temperature in the car. When we retrieved him later, the little crab was almost out of his shell, exposed, and nearly fried. I was so upset and knew we had to try and save him. So we placed him near the air conditioning unit in the hotel room, only to find him nearly frozen when we checked on him later. Do hermit crabs have nine lives? He rallied, and I could hardly wait to get him to the ocean so he could be happy and free.

The next day at the beach was the moment we had waited for. The little guy had survived an airplane ride and was nearly fried and frozen, all in the same day. He was going to be free to live his life in the ocean. We opened the box and the hermit crab ventured out. A breaking wave picked him up and quickly swept him into deeper water, but he seemed to be struggling. I stood there perplexed. What just happened? I thought he belonged in the ocean. "I think we drowned him, mom," Mike retorted. I was heartsick. My vacation was nearly ruined by this unhappy ending.

Later I related the story to my sister and her husband. He seemed not to be paying attention, but when I finished, he asked, "Did you keep the hermit in water here?" We had not. "Then why would you put him in the ocean?" he retorted. He's right. I did drown the little crab, even with the best intentions.

Ball games...so many ball games. Both of the boys played every seasonal sport in school. I think I could count on one hand the few games I missed due to work. I absolutely loved watching them play and excel in team sportsmanship. Their friends' parents became some of my closest friends. I was the boys' biggest fan in the stands.

One of our best memory makers was the basketball hoop in the driveway. I would play along with them. As the boys grew into teenagers, they would yell "foul" when I would jump on their backs when they had the ball or attempted to shoot a basket. That was the only way I could get the ball.

Our playing also included wrestling. When they were younger, I could wriggle out of their holds, but as they grew taller and stronger than me, I had to give them more for their money. Sometimes, I felt like a pretzel in those holds, but I rarely gave up. If I growled, I got stronger. The more they laughed at the growling, the weaker they grew, and sometimes I was able to free myself.

After growing up with three sisters, it was a refreshing adventure to raise boys. I taught them the rules of football, how to change the oil in a car (as my dad had taught me), and most importantly, how to be compassionate.

Their friends were always welcome, preferably when I was home. Now as adults, they have revealed that their friends would make a quick exit before 5:00 pm when I returned from work. But my motto was, "the more the merrier." They all called me

Momma Basil. I loved those days. We created such precious moments in those years, the three of us.

I often wished I had become a teacher, for more than one reason. I would have had the opportunity to spend summer days with Mike and Blake. And I would have avoided calls at work from the teenage babysitter, for example, advising me that the boys were on the roof of the house and would not come down. I guess at the ages of eight and ten, they wanted to view the world from up there. Luckily, I had the job flexibility to leave work mid-morning to come home and say, "Get your asses down now!" They had convinced the babysitter that I let them go on the roof all the time.

Another unforgettable event took place one morning as we were rushing through our usual routine. Blake handcuffed Mike's hands together just as we were walking out the door. He had purchased the handcuffs at a car show the weekend before, but the key was mysteriously missing. What do we do now? Mike could not go to school with his hands cuffed, but we were already going to be late for school and work. So we hurried to the nearest firehouse where the amused firemen decided to make the most of the occasion. They told Mike that they would have to use the "jaws of life" to free him. "You might lose your arm in the process," they teased him with serious faces. I will never forget his look of horror. Of course they removed the handcuffs without the "jaws of life" and without the loss of an arm, and we went on our way. Within an hour after arriving at work, I received a call from the principal to report that Mike had blackened Blake's eye.

It seemed like the blink of an eye that Mike was graduating from high school. I was so proud of him. He had already met the "love of his life" in his senior year. They dated a few years after high school before marrying. Dana is the daughter I never had. She is beautiful inside and out. Not long after the wedding they were living the American dream. Both of them were working, they were buying a house, and they adopted a chocolate lab named Rocky. Rocky was their first "baby," until they gave me three grandbabies within six years. I have such love in my heart and hope in my soul for their growing spirits.

6. Brady—The Child of a Child

Even before Mike married and started his family, we learned that his younger brother Blake, who was only sixteen and still in high school, was going to be a father. There's something unsettling about hearing for the first time that your child is expecting a child, and in this situation, it was exactly that.

The last thing I wanted for my youngest son was that he was going to be a father. What about high school? What about college? What about his future? How is he going to afford a baby? And WHO IS THE GIRL?

I went through so many emotions and questions. Where do we go from here? What do we do? There were attempts to come together with the family of the girl, who was also sixteen, but dealing with them became a living nightmare. It was their opinion that we were low-life, that Blake was totally to blame, and she was innocent.

Blake had requested that he at least be at the hospital when Brady was born, but we were not notified of his birth until hours afterwards. When we did receive the call, we rushed to the hospital and were greeted with cold stares and a piercing silence. This should be a joyous occasion, people! A healthy, baby boy has arrived in this world.

And the cold, hard looks and difficult relations continued for several years. The family maintained complete control and custody, allowing Blake no rights. We consistently requested visits with Brady at their convenience. Brady was Blake's son and my grandchild, but we were granted "approval" for only occasional half-hour visits with the child in their home. Those were precious moments, when we were able to hold him, talk to him, smile at him. When our time was up we would look forward to the next visit…whenever that may be.

From the beginning, Blake and I wanted to be a part of Brady's life. The door was slammed in our faces many times, but we never gave up hope. We never walked away. There were times it would have been less heartbreaking to throw up our hands, turn our backs, and walk away. But this little baby had a big piece of our hearts and he was going to be a part of our lives. We cherished our time with him. Through the many highs and lows of the next few years, there was one thing for sure: Blake loved his son, and Brady loved his daddy.

7. Casey

I have three younger sisters. Cassie, the one closest in age to me, is also my best friend. She and I have five sons between us, all close in age as well. Our two oldest sons, Mike and Larry, were six months apart. The middle boys, Blake and Casey, were seven months apart. And if it weren't for my miscarriage, her youngest son would have had a partner in crime. Needless to say, they all grew up together. When one mother wasn't there, the other one was. To this day, my sons call Aunt Cassie their second mom.

Mike, Blake, Larry, and Casey were the "fearless foursome." They were cousins who were as close as brothers. They had one another's backs and were best friends. For many years, they attended the same school together. What one didn't think of doing, another one did. To this day, I am in awe that my sister and I survived.

Blake and Casey grew to be the best buds. In high school, they began talking about their dreams. "We are going to get jobs and get an apartment together after graduation," they would exclaim. "We have plans."

In 2002, Casey's senior year, he came to live with Blake and me after Christmas break. Our home was closer to the high school, and I was able to take him to school in the morning. We had some good times and many laughs during those months. Most of the laughs were at my expense because of my incompetent cooking. Casey would say, "For the love of God, woman, how can anything edible come out of this kitchen?" I especially remember the hard, burnt chocolate cupcake that looked like it had been shellacked. When Casey dropped the cupcake and it thudded on the floor, he laughed heartily.

Casey began talking about spring break in Florida. "I am going to do it," he would say adamantly. There was no stopping him; he was on a mission. He was planning the trip with his friend, John, and he pleaded with Blake to go with them. On Easter Sunday, we celebrated as a family. That evening, Casey and John left for their trip south, but not before inviting Blake one more time. "I have to work bro," Blake reluctantly told him.

Casey had the time of his life that week on the beach. He took pictures of the ocean and texted Blake, "You should be here, dude, this is awesome. Can't you take a couple of days off work, fly down here, and we can drive back?" But Blake stayed home. "Gotta work and save for our apartment, man!" he answered.

Casey and John started the trip back on Friday evening. My sister was expecting a call from her son Saturday morning. Instead, at 9:00 am, she received the call that every parent dreads. It was from a hospital emergency room advising her that Casey had been in a horrible accident, just an hour from home. He had been driving all night and was tired, so John took over while Casey slept in the back seat. For some reason, John swerved off the road, causing the car to hydroplane and crash in a ditch. Casey sustained serious head trauma.

We all rushed to the hospital to find Casey unconscious, but without a scratch on him. "Please open those blue eyes, Casey, please" we pleaded. "He's going to be all right. He's going to be all right," we tried to reassure ourselves. I have never seen such worried, scared or shocked faces on my family. We were all felt so helpless; there was nothing we could do except pray. Casey's life was in the hands of the physicians...and God's.

For the next week, we stayed at the hospital praying for God's miracle. My sister rarely left Casey's bedside. If only he could open those piercing blue eyes. One day we saw a tear roll from Casey's left eye onto his cheek. We will never know if he heard our words, our prayers, our cries. Maybe this was the only way he could respond. Then we heard those awful words from the doctors. They echoed in the hospital room and felt like shards of glass stabbing our hearts. "There is no more we can do for Casey. The machines are keeping him alive." What do you mean there is no more hope?! Do you know how much Casey is loved? CASEY, GET UP!

Casey was a generous soul. He would always stick up for the underdog. He would give to someone in need. And on this last day of his life on earth, it was no different. He would be an organ donor. On Friday afternoon hospital staff made final preparations for that process. Shortly after 9:00 pm, we all said our final goodbyes to our beloved son, grandson, brother, nephew, best friend. The hall filled with the sounds of soft whimpering and not so soft cries that we will never forget. The nurses wheeled Casey out of his room—the room he had lain in for nearly a week; the room where many unanswered prayers were whispered. As he was slowly wheeled out of sight, I could see only the top of his head—his brown hair never to be stroked again. He was on his way to the surgical room to save three other lives with his gift of life. That week will be forever etched in our minds and hearts. Losing Casey has left a big empty space in our hearts, one that has never been filled.

Blake has questioned himself many times. The guilt and sadness overwhelmed him. What if he had joined them in Florida and drove them home? What if he had not called Casey to tell him of the party that Saturday night? Instead of rushing back, Casey would have started home on Saturday morning as planned. Cassie wondered, "What if I hadn't allowed him to leave?" We all have our "what if" questions and so many others that will never be answered.

A part of my sister also left with Casey. Her zest for life and her beautiful singing voice is silent. Since grade school, we had favorite songs we would sing together, but not anymore. Since Casey's death, she has lamented, "I have little to sing about."

I miss Casey. I miss my sister's songs.

8. Blake's Back Injury

Around the age of nineteen, Blake sustained a back injury at his job. He was prescribed pain medications and became more withdrawn. Doctors suggested surgery, pain management, and more pain pills. More pills. I watched helplessly as I put all my hopes in the doctors and the regimen of pills to cure my son's injury. As time went on, Blake became less motivated to do anything. He became addicted to the pain medications.

For Brady's safety, the mother and her family wanted Blake's visits supervised. After some time, we as a family were seeing Brady less and less. I missed my grandson. Would he remember how much he is loved? Would he remember me? "Please don't let me lose him, Lord," I prayed at night. I already felt I was losing my son; please, Lord, don't take my grandson.

There were many days and nights when I was overwhelmed with these emotions of fear, blame, and anger. The sheer feeling of hopelessness was sometimes just too much to bear. Blake agreed to participate in therapy at a couple of local rehabilitation centers. One rehab stay lasted four days and another for a couple of weeks. Blake also participated in out-patient services. Each rehab intervention was full of hope for a recovery.

Each recovery was followed by a relapse. It was time to pursue a long-term option for rehabilitation. It was the only hope we had remaining.

9. Mike's Back Injury

I am beginning to understand the meaning of "Never say never." My older son, Mike, the reliable family man, was my rock through Blake's addiction. He was the one I would call in the desperate hours of the night. He was the one whose words I hung onto with all the hope I could muster. If I knew anything, it was the guarantee that Mike would never succumb to the addiction of drugs or alcohol. Never say never.

Mike was at work one typical January morning in 2007 when one of the temporary cattle tie walls broke loose. In an instant, the scene turned into a dangerous situation for John, one of his co-workers, who was sweeping the floor beside it. If Mike had not reacted as he did, life could have turned out differently for this man. Mike saw the danger, ran over, and braced the wall with his back while John escaped. But Mike paid a price, sustaining an acute back injury. He had never experienced such excruciating pain in his life and was taken to the hospital for evaluation. That morning began a cycle of months of pain, inability to work, lack of motivation, and pain pills. Yes, pain pills. I had lost my "rock." My son, Mike, became addicted too. He voluntarily took himself to rehab twice. Thankfully, the second time around Mike got it, and he has never lost it.

10. Lull Before the Storm

For the next couple of years, our family felt like we were only hanging on. We survived life, rehabs, and relapses. I attended meetings of Al Anon, a support group for people dealing with loved ones with addictions. I remember a woman in one of those Al Anon meetings telling me, "Relapse is part of recovery." I wanted to slap her! Blake had just completed a week-long rehab, and he was healed! I remember we celebrated with a family dinner the day he came home to prove it. But relapse is exactly what happened more than once in the next two years.

Meanwhile, it seemed I was misplacing things more frequently. I blamed it on getting older and a failing memory, or that it was a result of having too much to think and worry about. I didn't carry much cash in my wallet and seldom knew exactly how many dollar bills I had in my purse. Many times I thought I had an extra five dollars, but I couldn't remember where I had spent it. That was because I had not spent it.

One fall evening, Blake, Brady, and I had built a campfire in the back yard. The two of them were laughing and making s'mores. Thinking that it was a perfect "Kodak moment," I ran inside to get my camera. I couldn't find it in the usual place and searched everywhere in the house. I was frantic. I had misplaced my expensive camera. Blake called out, "Mom, don't worry about taking a picture. Let's enjoy the moment." He did not want me looking for the camera because he knew I wouldn't find it. He had pawned it. With this realization, my heart sank deeper than I thought possible.

One day Blake called me while he was out of town saying he had an awful toothache and had found a dentist who would fix it. He frantically asked me to wire him $200 for the dental bill. I did. To this day, I have never asked if that was a true story. I just don't want to know.

Sometimes a gut feeling or a voice in my head would tell me that my son was "using" again, but when I asked him if had taken money or a valuable to pawn, pleading for the truth, I would believe his denials. He would look me straight in the eye and convincingly say, "No mom, I didn't take any money from your purse," or "No mom, I don't know where your ring is." All the while, I am going nuts. Did I have that $20 in my wallet? Did I lose my special ring? Stealing from me was not a concept I could wrap my heart around.

11. Blake's Intervention

In September 2007, just before the intervention, things were changing fast, spiraling down. I knew in my gut that my son was not in a good place. I began the search for a more intensive rehabilitation facility. Every attempt to this point had been unsuccessful. We had been to hell and back for several years. I was growing desperate. Blake was slipping through our fingers. The family members seldom heard from him anymore, including his own son.

I woke up one Friday morning (I am not sure I slept that night) and felt a fear like I have never experienced before. It took over my whole body. "My son was in grave danger," I heard silently, and I felt it in my heart. I began to look on the Internet for long-term rehabilitation programs. I remember my search did not take long. It was as if I had someone working with me every step. Within hours, I spoke to a referral agency, a counselor from the rehab program, and an interventionist. Before my next thought, the intervention was scheduled for Friday evening. That evening! They told me to pack a suitcase for my son. The interventionist was leaving and would be in our home in four hours.

That afternoon, I received a call from Blake. He said, "I'm all right, mom. I've rented a room at the D & D Motel across town." The voice on the other end of the phone was NOT my son. But it WAS him. I wanted to keep him talking…about something… anything. But he only said, "I love you, mom, always remember that," and then CLICK. CLICK...he was gone. Oh my God. I was so numb I could only pace, five feet in one direction and five feet back. Repeat. It became my ritual for the rest of that day, evening, and night. I felt like a caged animal.

When the interventionists arrived in town, we gathered at my parents' home. My sister and Mike were also present. Ben and Sharon introduced themselves. They began to speak of the disease. The word "enabling" was brought to the table. Suddenly, I felt all eyes on me. "What do you mean, enabling? I just love Blake and would do anything for him." There were the words! "I would do anything for him." Damn right I would! God help the person who tries to stand in my way. Ben said to me, "Do you realize that when you enable him, you are not helping him, and you are feeding the addiction? He knows he has you to always be there to pick him up." I looked at him with piercing eyes and said, "I will not stand back and watch this addiction kill my son. I will not!"

Mike looked at me and gently said, "Mom, Blake's addiction is killing YOU. I cannot stand back and watch YOU slip away from us. You always look exhausted. You live and breathe Blake's addiction." Once again Mike told me I was attempting to put a Band-aid over a bleeding artery. One of the most challenging and heartbreaking experiences in Mike's life was watching the addiction take over his brother's life. He couldn't protect his brother from the choking effects of this disease any more than he could take away the pain in his mother's heart. I began to cry. The last thing I ever want to do is hurt either of my sons.

The interventionists continued their process. We were all asked to write a letter "from the heart" to Blake. There was a plan. "We will meet again tomorrow. We will review your letters, and we will find Blake," Ben said.

We all went our separate ways around 10:00 pm. I was mentally and emotionally exhausted, but I stayed up half the night writing my letter. The other half, I worried. "Please let the angels watch over Blake tonight," I prayed over and over.

When daybreak finally arrived, I was already up, pacing five feet forward and back. I attempted to pack Blake's suitcase, but I could barely see what I was doing for the tears in my eyes. Part of me was overwhelmed with a feeling of deceit while I packed his belongings. On the other hand, I hoped with all my heart that this was going to save his life.

With letter in one hand and suitcase in the other, I went to meet Ben and Sharon at Mike's house. Blake's dad, Taylor was also present that day. Ben and Sharon spoke of the bottom line. What was this bottom line? They explained, "Once you read your letters, and if he doesn't accept treatment NOW, you will no longer enable his life as an addict." There was that term again…ENABLING, and once again, I felt all eyes on me. I guess everyone was in agreement at this point that I was the biggest enabler in the room. Mike, spoke to me again from his heart. "Mom, when you help Blake, it's like putting a Band-Aid over a bleeding artery." Oh my God! I got that. (And how did he get so smart?) Reluctantly, I agreed to the bottom line. I was the last one.

Mike had been in contact with Blake the night before and had asked him to come over that afternoon. This was part of the intervention plan, but Blake did not show. He did not answer his cell phone. Dear Lord, please let him be alive.

At mid-afternoon, we formed a caravan including my parents, Mike, Taylor, Cassie and I, and the interventionists, and drove to the other side of town to confront Blake. When we pulled up to the D & D Motel, I felt nauseated. My son was HERE? A warm sensation rushed through my body, and yet I was shaking like I was without a coat on a cold day. From the looks of the setting, we were not in a good place. What was Blake doing HERE? We walked together up to the door of the one-room apartment. Blake was supposedly on the other side.

I was the first one to the door. I knocked. No answer. I knocked harder and harder, crying Blake's name. Ben was standing beside me, coaxing me with words to say. There was a window to the side of the door, and I saw the curtain move. Suddenly, I heard Blake's voice. I heard Blake say, "Go away." The words seemed to linger in the air.

I knocked harder; I pleaded more. "Blake, please open this door." One by one, each family member went to the door and tried their persuasion. Ben, the expert, also tried, but to no avail. We stood outside that door for an hour waiting for a miracle. At last Blake said, "Only Mike and mom can come in." Everyone else waited patiently outside, even the interventionists.

I walked in, and for the second time that day, I felt like I was going to be sick. The room was dark and gloomy. The place was a disaster. Blake was a disaster. He sat on the couch and gazed at me with a faraway look in his eyes. He told us he wanted to die and this was the place he had chosen to do it.

Mike got in Blake's face and calmly but firmly told him, "On the other side of that door are family members who care about you, and the least you could do is let them tell you how much they care and tell you goodbye." Blake listened to Mike, as I have seen him do so many times throughout the years. If there was anyone Blake would listen to, it was his brother. They have an understanding like that.

So Blake said reluctantly, "Let them in." One by one, Blake's grandparents, father, aunt, and the interventionists came in. Ben orchestrated the intervention by asking us to read our letters to Blake, beginning with me.

"Dear Blake," I began. "You are my youngest son. I love you very much. I remember you as a young child and that shit-eating grin! Sometimes, I still see that grin! I remember when you were five years old, and you had to have a rabbit for your birthday! You named him Spanky, and you cared for him every day. No one in the family was in favor of you having a rabbit. But I saw how happy you were caring for Spanky, and it was the right decision to get the rabbit for you.

"I remember when you, Mike, and I would sit down for

dinners and when it was springtime, you two would gulp down your food and fly outside to play, but not until you put your arm around my neck, and we would say together, 'darling, I simply adore you!' I can still see that little face. Blake, we share similar loves, such as the full moon, the ocean, and the wonder of them both. You know when I am hurt, and you say the right things.

"I remember when you were about nine years old, and you saw me upset about the death of one of the residents at my work. You put your arm around me and said, 'Don't cry mommy. Johnny is up in heaven, running, riding his bike, and laughing.' I carry that story in my heart always. Thanks for being there for me.

"But for some time now, there have been changes. It seems that you are withdrawing from the family. When we have family gatherings, you don't participate. People ask about you, people care about you. There have been incidences of stealing and lying, incidences that could have had much bigger consequences. When I see you spend each day, week, month spinning your wheels, breaking promises to yourself and others, it is heart wrenching to watch.

"I want my son back. I want to hear you laugh and see that familiar grin. I want you to feel the peace and love in that generous heart in your chest. I love you, Blake. Will you please accept some help? Love, Mom"

There was not a dry eye in that God-awful room. Blake began to cry uncontrollably on his brother's shoulder. Mike looked at him and said, "This is it, bro. Now, or never." Blake looked up at his brother and said, "I WILL GO." Within minutes, we were on our way. We walked to Ben's car. I brought the packed suit-case from my car. One by one, each family member embraced Blake.

I hugged my son with all my might. I was holding on for dear life, but the words would not come. What can I say to him, right now? I had so much to say, yet nothing would come out of my mouth. Blake was in Ben's car with the out-of -state tags. The car pulled away. I saw Blake's hand rise in a faint wave.

I watched the tail lights fade in the darkness. I said to my sis-ter, without taking my eyes off the car, "I just sent my son away to a place I have never seen with two people I just met yesterday. What the heck did I just do?"

The ride home was quiet. I felt like I had been punched in the stomach. At the same time, I felt overwhelming relief. My son was alive and on his way to get help.

One thing I did know; I was exhausted. We all were exhausted. I asked Ben to call me when they arrived at the rehab center. Four hours later, at 3:00 am, I received the call. Blake had arrived safely. Now it was time to rest my head on the pillow.

12. My Journal During Blake's Rehab

Day #3

I really do not know what to feel since Blake left in that car a few nights ago. There are so many emotions. I think I am mostly numb. It is as if life is going on all around me, and I am watching it from a distance. I am going through the motions, going to work and trying to sleep at night. I do know I feel gratitude in my heart for the little things. I watched squirrels in the trees for the longest time, just appreciating nature. There seems to be a little peace in my soul.

Day #4

A counselor from the center called for Blake's mom with a message from him. Tell mom I love her very much. That message went straight to my heart.

Day #5

Blake called! He has finished the withdrawal/detox segment. He described detox as rough. He is not sleeping at night; he stares at the ceiling.

Day #7

Blake sounded very down tonight on the phone. He says he wants to use.

Day #8

Blake opened up tonight. He said he really thought he was going to die in that motel room, and that his family would be better off without him. He said when he was in that motel room, using drugs, when he looked in the mirror, he saw a skeleton face staring back at him. "Mom, it was my face. I felt death all around me." I thought of my intuition the day before his intervention. It makes some sense now. It was God who directed me to those interventionists. There will never be a doubt in my heart about that. Thank God, I listened. From this day forward, I will never have qualms about the money spent for Blake's recovery....It could have been his funeral.

Day #15

Blake said, "The weeks go fast, the days drag."

Day #16

Blake and I had our first disagreement. Sauna (part of the intense detoxification) is making him tired. Real tired. The counselor said, "He will have mood changes the next week or so."

Day #17

"Sauna is kicking my butt," but he says he feels good! Blake talked to his son today.

Day #18

Blake is down.

Day #19

"Today was the best day ever, mom!" He sounded so good. He said he talked two students into staying in the program. I told him I was so proud of him. "The reason," he said, "is because of the way you raised me, mom." I slept peacefully tonight.

Day #20

Blake said the team leaders are depending on Blake to help other students. I reminded him that you and your recovery are #1. He misses Brady.

Day #21

Brady was spending the night at Gramie's, and Blake talked to him. It was very emotional for both of them. Blake could barely say goodbye after he talked to Brady. God bless him.

Day #22

Blake was down today. I could hear it in his voice. "Keep your head up," I cried when we hung up. I miss him very much. What I wouldn't do to kiss his head. I know he is in a safe place, a place to get all the drugs out of him. I know he misses Brady.

Day #23

He wants learn to play the guitar! He wants to go to Greece with one of his roommates. At least, he has dreams now.

Day #24

Brady sent his daddy a note and drawings. The counselor reported that Blake is doing "phenomenal."

Day #25

"I feel awesome!" Blake said. He's smiling.

Day #26

I hear Blake's sense of humor again. I love that sense of humor!

Day #27

He was the DJ in the fashion show. He said graduation was emotional. It was not his graduation.

Day #28

We talked about the last four weeks and how much he's changed. I asked him what he remembered of that time, and he said, "Death was all around me." Oh my God.

Day #29

He said this was his first good Sunday. "Most Sundays here are very depressing," He said, "I feel great."

Day #30

"Long day, mom."

Day #31

Blake said, "Hard to think of all the time I have to go yet, but I am committed to finishing the program."

Day #32

"I will probably stay at the center and work after my program. I am afraid I will use when I come home. I want to come home a clean, successful man."

Day #33

I miss my son.

Day #34

This mom has some serenity now.

Day #35

What was his happiest moment of the day? Today he said, "My

good mood. I see all the bullshit in life, and I don't want to play the games anymore."

Day #36

Blake can have visitors next Sunday. He wants to see me, his dad, and his brother. Then he said, "Seeing you, mom, and then you leaving will be the hardest for me; maybe you could wait till I finish the program." I told him, "Whatever you want to do is fine with me." God bless him.

Day #37

The leader said today he's going to make sure Blake gets it. I thank God every day for showing the path. Blake was laughing on the phone with his buddies. It's so good to hear his laugh again.

Day #38

Blake sounded down or tired today. The ethics counselor wrote an awesome letter about Blake being a model student. Blake was proud.

Day #39

Blake said he's "learning to learn, and it's hard to concentrate that much."

Day #40

Learning to study, and he gets pissed off. He couldn't get it. But the counselor stayed with him and helped Blake get it. His best moment today was getting it.

Day #41

He called when the family was heading to our annual out-of-state football game. His voice dropped. He talked to his son.

Day #44

Blake had his first family visit today. His dad and brother went to see him. I thought it best for me to wait for our visit.

Day #45

What is your happiest moment today, and he said, "Katie telling me she would marry me." (Who's Katie?!)

Day #46

Blake talked to Brady tonight. He really misses him...he really misses him.

Day #49

I got to see my son today. First visit since he left that dreadful Sunday evening. I couldn't believe my eyes when I saw him through the window. I ran like a school child to the front door and wrapped my arms around his neck. He hugged me as hard as I hugged him. He has gained ten pounds and has muscles! We sat and talked for four and a half hours! We haven't had a conversation like this for a very long time. It was my son talking and not the drugs. He really looks healthy. It was very hard to leave him...real hard...but I didn't cry in front of him. I cried driving back home.

Day #51

There were twelve people who arrived on the doorsteps of the rehab facility the same time Blake did. Blake is the only one who continues to work the program...the only one of twelve. I pray he gets through it. I cannot help him now.

Day #56

Blake is really down. He said, "The only reason I haven't started walking home is because of Brady."

Day #57

Today when I asked Blake what his happiest moment was, he said, "It was nothing."

Day #65

Ten days have passed with no message from Blake.

Day#66

Blake's smile is back. I heard it in his voice. Blake missed roll call, so the consequence is no visitors on Sunday.

Day #67

Thanksgiving Day...the family was in a circle, getting ready to say what we are thankful for when Blake called on the phone. We all chimed in to say "Happy thanksgiving, Blake!" I had the biggest lump in my throat.

Day #70

Several family members took off in the motor home for a trip to Michigan. I was so excited to see Blake's face. Within the hour, I got a call from Mike while I was visiting with Blake. He said, "Mom, one of Blake's friends (Joe) was in a car accident last night, alcohol related. He didn't survive." I am sitting beside Blake. Mike told me not to tell Blake. Blake could tell by my face, something bad had happened. And he didn't stop asking what was wrong. I couldn't lie to him. I will never forget the look on his face. He shook with every fiber in his being. He tried to hold back the uncontrollable tears. Joe was with Blake in the hotel room that awful Sunday night. Joe talked Blake out of a lot of things that night. One of them was suicide. Blake looked at me and said, "Why Joe, mom? Why not me?" God help us all.

Day #73

Blake wanted to use bad today. He is dealing with unmasked/unmedicated pain. He is trying to keep his heart and mind on course. He wanted to be at Joe's funeral today.

Day #80

During a phone call, I asked Blake how he was. He said, "shitty." "Don't know if I am going to finish this, mom."

Day #83

Today, I was at another rehab facility with my oldest son. Mike was being admitted… addicted to pain medication. Dear God.

Day #87

Brady is with me today. I have so much fun with him. I know he misses his daddy. Today I picked up Mike from the rehab center. He was ready to go home. When we arrived at his house, his wife and children were waiting at the door for him, smiling from ear to ear. His children grabbed onto his legs and wouldn't let him go. I quietly put his bag inside the door and left. God be with Mike and give him direction.

Day #100

I just got home from the drive to Michigan with my sister. We visited Blake. It was so good to see him. There was a definite calmness about him.

Christmas Day

We are such a close family. I have never spent Christmas away from my sons, but today I did. We all missed him so much. Blake is such a big part of this family. Brady asked, "Will daddy be here next Christmas?" He said, "I want to spend that Christmas with my daddy."

New Year's Day

Finally, 2007 is over. We made it through the holidays. Blake said, "I didn't watch the ball drop at midnight." Neither did I.

Day #112

"I know what is right, mom…and I am not scared."

Day #116

I love to hear him laugh. That laugh was dormant for many months.

Day #135

A couple of family members spent the afternoon together in the center's visiting room with Blake. It's awesome to see you smile and laugh. You played with the children who were visiting their daddies and mommies in the same room. Any child's eyes light up when you give them attention. Children love to be around you…always has been that way. That's one of the reasons Brady is so blessed to have you as his daddy. It was difficult to leave you tonight. I just wanted to say, "Come on, Blake, we are going home."

Day #139

Blake has completed all the objectives and goals for the program to graduate. Congratulations, Blake. He is very proud. What an accomplishment. Blake is going back to the Center and work as a trainee after his rehab.

Day #148

As part of the program, Blake asked me what I wanted from him. "To be happy, successful, honest, and clean," I said. And what did I need from him? "To be happy and honest…and humorous." He then apologized for all the hurt he caused while using drugs. Thank you Blake, for that gift of sincerity and honesty.

Day #152

You are on the home stretch now! You have helped so many other people while you were in rehab. I am so happy you are coming home for a little while….I know you need to go back, and I support that decision 100 percent. I have missed you these past five months. Well, I have missed "you" for quite a few years now.

Day #153

At 3:10 pm this afternoon, Blake called me at work and said, "I did it, mom. I finished the program. I got a 95 percent on my final exam." I couldn't be more proud of you, my son. And when we hung up, I got down on my knees and thanked God for this miracle.

Day #154

Well, Blake, this is the last note I will be writing, charting your course in the program. For most of the last 154 days I have written a note. I appreciated your phone calls. I so looked forward to hearing your voice. I won't sleep much tonight, because I will be ready for the sun to rise, so I can head up to that "state up north" to watch you get your certificate. Then we will bring you home for a few days. I know you have worked hard and long for the past five months. You are positively a different person and young man. I pray that you continue on this path of sobriety, honesty, success, and happiness for the rest of your life. I will always pray for your strength to not return to the addiction. You have it, you got it, and you have earned it. NOW LIVE IT. I am proud of you. Tomorrow night, you will rest your head under this roof.

All is well.

Love,

Momma

13. Graduation Day

There was a lot of rushing about getting ready for the trip this morning. Too much rushing around, as I came to realize later in the day. We had just enough time to make the trip for the graduation ceremony.

Before I left, I went to the favorite chair of my cat, Tigger, that I've had for sixteen years, to tell him I would be back. When I picked him up to hug him, I realized his breathing was labored, and he let out a painful meow. What was the matter with my Tigger? I knew something was very wrong. I had to take him to the vet, NOW. Since I rescued him as a small kitten, he had never been sick. Why today? Why now?

Other family members convinced me there was no time to take Tigger to the vet. They made arrangements and one of them took Tigger to the vet. I was frightened. I asked her to put the phone on speaker while she spoke to the doctor. I could hear my pet crying in a meowing chant I had never heard before today. I knew he was frightened and in pain. After the appointment, she did not hang up the phone, and I could hear Tigger crying on the way home. Then there was silence…no more meowing. I thought to myself, thank goodness he has calmed down. I will hold him when I get back home tonight.

All afternoon, I received no call from home regarding Tigger. Fifteen minutes before the graduation was to begin, I sneaked out the side door to make a call. Finally someone picked up. I did not anticipate the reaction on the other end. "No one told you?" Told me what? My little Tigger was gone. He died on the way home...when I heard him become silent.

I walked back into the center and sat down. The ceremony was about to begin. I was shaking from the inside out. Blake looked at me and said, "God, mom, are you crying already?" He had no idea about Tigger, this cat he has loved for sixteen of his twenty-four years. I wasn't going to tell him then.

I have never had the experience of feeling such deep sadness and overwhelming joy all at the same time. My long-time pet had died and my son had successfully completed a five-month recovery program, all in the same day. What a day.

14. More Setbacks

In the same month that Blake graduated from his rehabilitation program, he found out that Mike was using again, and now it was Blake's turn to help his brother. Blake and Mike's wife, Dana, confronted him about their suspicions that he was taking pills again. God bless Mike. Let him know he does not have to do this alone. I hate drugs, I hate pills, and I hate alcohol. I hate all of it and the devastation it brings to lives and families. Blake took him to rehab again. I pray Mike gets it this time.

The day of our court date arrived—a hearing to bring Brady back in our lives. I prayed that we would be able to see Brady. I wanted a good relationship with my grandson and one for him with his daddy too. I had not given up yet and didn't plan to. Sadly, no decision was made at court.

I took Blake back to Michigan yesterday. When I returned home, I went straight to my bedroom, physically and emotionally exhausted, to find a box on the bed. I didn't know what it was. Opening, it, I found it held the ashes of my little Tigger cat, and I started to cry. All the emotions of losing my beloved pet, Blake graduating and leaving again, and Mike returning to rehab were about all I could handle.

Later, Blake came home for a couple of weeks, and then returned to the rehab center in Michigan for training to work as an employee at the facility. He was returning to rehab to "pay it back" and help others see a ray of hope in their addiction.

A sense of peace settled in during that summer. Mike was successful in his recovery and Blake was working at the treatment center. The serenity did not go unnoticed or unappreciated. Towards the end of summer, Blake was spending more time at home. He got a job working forty hours a week, and things appeared to be going well. Life was carrying on for all of us.

But by September, that God-awful, yet familiar feeling of knowing, but not wanting to believe returned in the pit in my stomach. I thought I was going crazy—misplacing money, my camera, and ring. That heart-wrenching fear of suspicion crept back again. I prayed to God that it was not true, that my gut, heart, and mind were wrong.

I was not losing things. Blake had stolen them to feed his addiction. I was enabling Blake again; I wanted to protect him. Mike was aware of the old habits returning and said to me, "I am pulling away from you, mom, so it won't be so painful when you have a heart attack over Blake's addiction. I don't want to go through this with Blake anymore, and I am ready to kick his ass."

One year and thousands of dollars later, we were heading down the same road. I did not know what hurt the most, my stomach or my heart.

15. The Beating

We celebrated Christmas and the 2010 New Year with fresh starts and high hopes. I was trying to believe that all would be well. The past year had brought another roller coaster of emotions. I wanted so desperately to believe Blake's words were true, but in my gut, I felt something else. I tried to have a short conversation with Blake on a daily basis. It was the way I knew he was alive and functioning.

I woke up one morning barely into the new year thinking I'd had a nightmare. I had talked to Blake on the phone, and he was obviously drugged up. It was no nightmare; it was true. I didn't know what to feel any more. I wanted to believe and hope that Blake would get his life together and get off the pills. How could he go back to the pills? I will never understand addiction as long as I live and breathe. Blake had relapsed and I needed to let go and let God. I needed to stay in my own space. Blake told me, "Mom, you need drama." Maybe he was right. He was basically telling me to let him live his own life. I needed to do that. I needed to take a deep breath, take my dog for a walk, and get to an Al-anon meeting.

January 11 began like any other day. The workday was extremely busy, for which I was thankful. It kept my mind focused. Throughout the day, Blake crossed my mind, as he often did. I called and left a message on his cell phone later in the afternoon. Before I left work, I received a call from Brady's mother asking if I had talked to Blake that day. He had not returned her calls, and Brady wanted to talk to him. Blake rarely missed a call to talk to Brady. I became a little concerned. I called his cell again; there was still no answer.

On the way home, my thoughts and heart were racing. I had that all-too-familiar gut feeling that something was wrong with Blake. I tried on my own to reassure myself that he was all right. I was not succeeding. Within an hour, I made phone calls to family who might have seen or talked to Blake that day.

I called Cassie. "Something is wrong with Blake," I said. I never have to mince words with my sister; I can just blurt it out. She assured me that he was just not answering his phone and that he was all right. I am usually comforted by her words, but not this night.

I called Blake's cell phone again and this time it went straight to voice mail. I left a message, "Blake, please call momma. Just let me know you are all right."

I called Blake's father. He said to me, as he typically does, "Blake is an adult, he is all right."

I called Mike. "Mom, when are you going to stop killing yourself with this worry? Blake is okay." We hung up.

I was in the car, but I did not even know where I was driving. Suddenly I felt so alone. There was no one I could turn to who understood my level of heart-wrenching fear. I felt so helpless, alone, and scared to death. I prayed over and over, "Please Lord, let Blake be all right."

Darkness came and still there was no word from Blake. I called one more time. Blake's phone had no ring, no voice mail and no voice message. It was turned OFF.

I walked down the driveway. I began my pacing, five feet forward, about face, and five feet back. I was shaking violently. I did not know if it was the cold winter air or my insides turned inside out. I felt in every fiber of my being that Blake was in grave danger. If I closed my eyes, I envisioned him lying in a field with blood covering his face. I couldn't close my eyes. I just looked up at the heavens and sobbed uncontrollably.

By 10:00 pm, I wondered how I could get through the night. I went inside and lay across my bed. I felt as if my body and mind were not connected anymore. I couldn't get the bad thoughts out of my head, and I certainly wasn't able to control my body. Before I realized it, I was lying in a fetal position. Every muscle in my body was moving involuntarily. I felt as if I was in severe physical pain, and I couldn't find a painless body position.

Then my cell phone rang. I grabbed it and answered before the first ring had completed.

On the other end I heard, "This is Officer Smith from the police department. Is this Pam Basil?" I summoned all my strength to answer, "Yes, is my son all right?"

"Yes, he is currently with me and he will need some medical attention, as he was kidnapped and beaten. He escaped with his life. He is very lucky to be alive," the officer said.

He escaped with his life...he escaped with his life!

The kidnapping remained a question mark, as the family never learned the details. But during the next several weeks, Blake recovered from a fractured nose and bruises about his face and his back. It was heartbreaking to see the belt marks across his back. Worst of all were the horrific nightmares he would have. Every time he closed his eyes he could imagine another blow to the face.

It had been hell...for all of us. Blake was fortunate that his physical injuries were limited to a broken nose and belt marks. The emotional wounds were much bigger. He couldn't sleep, couldn't eat, or close his eyes without the nightmares returning.

Never before in my life had I experienced such level of anxiety and fear, and neither had Blake. He told me that while he was bound and gagged in that wooden chair, his cell phone would ring. He knew on the other end of the call was someone who cared about him. When the kidnapper turned the phone off, Blake said to himself, "That is my last contact with my family forever."

In the aftermath, I was barely holding on. I needed to realize that I could control only my own attitude and set my own boundaries. I feel so low, so worn down. Even though Blake experienced the physical beating, I felt as if my body and heart had gone through something similar.

My oldest son came to see me while Blake was still recovering. Mike talked of fears of losing his momma. "I am having dreams that my mom is going to have a heart attack," he confided.

"Mom, Blake is your drug of choice. You are addicted to his surviving his addiction." He's probably right. I cannot protect Blake 24/7. God will.

So Mike called a family gathering. He told his father and me that he needed to get some things off his chest; his heart was heavy. Mike said, "Blake is crying out for help." He strongly believed his brother needed to go back to rehab. I believe God spoke through Mike. It was God who gave us the tools and insight to stand up to this disease…once again.

That afternoon, Blake, his dad and I drove to a nearby park. We were open and honest with Blake. We expected a lot of resistance from him, but quite the opposite occurred. Almost like a scolded puppy, Blake said, "I will do whatever is best."

Nearly two and half years had passed since Blake's graduation from the program, and here we were—going through round two. Blake apparently did some soul searching after his horrific experience and took the opportunity to try the rehab program one more time.

The next morning, Blake agreed to head back north to the rehab center. Before we left, he said his goodbyes to his grandparents, his brother…and his son. My heart ached for the two of them.

As he entered the doors to the rehab center, he remarked, "I'm a re-tread." A re-tread. That's the term used for this second time around. I hugged his neck, kissed his cheek, and said goodbye once again. I drove home in a mental fog. I didn't know how I felt, what to think, or what to say out loud to myself. So I just prayed.

16. Round Two Rehab

My journal entries starting in February 2010:

Day #3

I am beginning to feel less numb today. My chest feels lighter, my left arm doesn't ache as much, and I cried less tears. I made it a "gratitude day." I just thanked God for everything all day long. It made a difference. Just one day at a time.

Day #9

I am really working on staying out of the way this time around.

Day #10

My son is alive. He survived that kidnapping. The peace of Blake being alive and safe has penetrated my soul today.

Day #15

Blake called today and asked for forgiveness for his wrongdoings during his using. He asked for re-entry into the family. I accepted and said, "Your family has never left you." We never lost hope.

Day #16

"Mom, could you send up some of my dress clothes? I am going to take training classes."

Day #18

Brady made a basket at his game today! He can't wait to call and tell his daddy!

Day #26

Yesterday was Brady's tenth birthday. He misses his daddy, but Brady has 364 days to be ten and to see his dad.

Day #32

At 2:20 pm, I am picking up Brady at school, and we are heading up north to visit his dad. Brady is so very excited!

Day #34

I had no idea what was in store for us on the way back from the visit with Blake. The weekend was full of time spent with Blake doing fun things and laughing our heads off. But the goodbye for Brady was almost unbearable to watch. And the hardest part was listening to my grandson sobbing in the back seat with a pillow covering his face. When he dropped the pillow from his face, he would look at me with sad eyes, and say, "Why can't my daddy come home?" I tried my best to explain to a child the devastation of addiction and the hope of recovery. It broke my heart.

Day #37

Blake talked to the administrator about observing interventions. The sky is the limit for Blake as long as he remains clean. In the past few weeks, Blake has been clean and helping others at the center. One of the owners sees the possible potential in Blake and his skills. Blake has been shadowing the interventionist.

Day #44

This disease has taken another heart of gold. We learned that our cousin, Robby, died in a car accident. Alcohol was involved. Both the driver and Robby were killed. God bless them and their families.

Day #72

Blake got a recommendation letter from a district manager at the rehab center. One sentence in the letter was as follows: "Blake, you are helping save lives."

Day #81

Brady now sleeps with two little stuffed bears. Clover and Lucky never made it out of the suitcase when he was with his dad this weekend. I imagine the security of his dad's presence was all he needed.

Day #103

I am sitting on the side of the bed watching my grandson sleep so peacefully. I have to wake him up now to eat cinnamon rolls (his favorite!) and go to school.

For several months, Blake has been travelling from state to state doing interventions. He is making a difference in families affected by addiction. The moms want to "adopt" Blake, and he has been offered a place to stay with these families if he vacations in that state. The level of trust is unbelievable.

Day #105

Happy birthday Blake. I believe this is the first birthday I have not been able to give you a birthday hug. Have a great birthday.

Day #112

I lost a good friend today. She was full of life and her life ended today. Out of the blue, Brady called this evening and wanted to spend the night. He did, and he made me smile a hundred times. I asked him, "How did you know Gramie needed you tonight?" I told him he was a life saver. Bless his heart.

Day #136

It's Saturday morn, still dark, and the birds are singing. Blake and his dad got to spend the day and evening together yesterday. That's a good thing. Just the two of them…it has been a long time coming. I hope it filled some empty spaces in your heart, Blake.

Day #140

Last night, I saw little Brady smile from ear to ear. He could barely talk; he was smiling so big! He got to pitch in his baseball game! After he pitched a great game, he ran over to me and asked, "Can we call my dad?"

Day #142

I mentioned about coming to see you this Sunday with Brady. You really didn't say one way or another.

Day #148

Brady and I won't be making the trip to see you. You said you had to work.

Day #151

It's July 4th. Last evening, I was sitting with Brady watching the fireworks. A part of you was there.

Day #153

This chapter is closed…something happened in Michigan… something happened to you…not sure you are clean, not sure you still have your intervention job, not sure of anything right now.

Blake relapsed. He lost his job.

Day #155

You used. I won't be writing in this journal anymore.

17. Surgery, Relapse, and Tough Love

After the second rehab, on day #154, Blake relapsed. He came home for a little while and continued to use. He knew his only option was to return to rehab. He did go back to Michigan, but did not go to rehab. He just wasn't using at home. There were times I did not talk to him, and I had no idea where he was. I knew in my heart that it was not good. He would call every once in a while and tell me, "mom, I am okay; don't worry," but I knew he was not okay at all. I felt completely powerless.

One Friday afternoon, I had errands to run at lunch. I bought a box of junior mints and ate almost all of them. I got back to work, and my stomach began to hurt. I thought to myself, "Wow, I should not have eaten all that candy." After a couple of hours, the pain in my stomach worsened severely. I thought I just needed to go home and lie down. Resting didn't help. My sister called, and she could tell immediately in my voice that something was wrong. She told me, "I am coming over."

By the time she arrived, I was vomiting and the pain was severe. She noticed my lips were white and insisted on taking me to the ER. I told her, "I am not going to the ER for eating too many junior mints, and my lips are white because of the mints."

She didn't buy it. Soon I was in the back seat of the car in severe pain…pain I had never experienced before.

Ironically, on the way to the hospital, Blake called my cell phone and asked me to pick him up in Michigan. I couldn't even talk. I didn't want to talk. I wanted someone to take away this pain before it killed me, or I killed someone else.

I sat in the ER for what seemed like an eternity. I remember threatening the nurse, "You either give me some medicine for pain or a gun." Thankfully, I got the pain medicine. A doctor came in and pressed on my stomach. If I hadn't been semi-sedated, I would have punched him. "Yes, she has an acute appendicitis," the doctor told my family. I was admitted to the hospital and spent a horrendous night. I had to wait until the next morning for my appendix and me to go our separate ways.

I lay in the pre-surgery room with my two sons on either side of me. Blake's dad had made the trip to Michigan the night before to bring him home. I couldn't wait to get rid of this appendix. I remember my boys trying to make me laugh by telling "mom" stories to the nursing staff in the pre-op room. Although they tried their best not to show it, they were scared. I was scared. Surgery went well, but it was a slow recovery time. I spent nearly a week in the hospital. I could not even think of food although my family kept coaxing me to eat. I would eat and vomit.

When I got home all I wanted to do was lie in bed. I tried to sleep most of the time, mainly to escape worrying about Blake, because he had returned to Michigan. He did make it back to the rehab center.

After a couple of weeks, I called the rehab center to inquire about Blake. The lady who answered the phone was aloof when I identified myself. "I will have a counselor return your call," she said nervously. I asked, "Is my son all right?" and she would only repeat, "I will have a counselor call you." "When?" I asked. "Is my son all right?" I knew in my gut something else had happened. Long minutes passed that seemed like hours, but no one called me back, so I called the center again. "Please, just let me know my son is okay," I pleaded, to no avail.

Finally a new, young counselor called me to report, "Your son is no longer here." "What? Where is he?" Dom, one of the head chiefs at the center, instructed their transport to take Blake to a homeless shelter…to a parking lot…to a dump…he didn't care where. So Blake opted to go to a Walmart parking lot with his six garbage bags of belongings.

After a little while, I received a call from Blake. "Mom, can you pick me up?" I asked him what had happened. "Mom, Dom just went berserk and told me to leave. I am in a Walmart parking lot. Can you please come get me?"

Any physical recovery I had made had just gone out the window. I was literally sick to my stomach. Do I go get Blake? Do I leave him in Detroit, Michigan in a Walmart parking lot? I started contacting people: an Al-Anon friend; my best friend's husband, who is an attorney; my sister; anyone who could tell me what to do. Of course, no one told me what to do, but the general underlying feeling was that this is where tough love comes into play.

I paced the floor, my five steps forward and back, trying to make a decision. I closed my eyes, and pictured the dark night and Blake in that parking lot in Detroit Michigan. I grabbed my car keys, still in my house dress (really pajamas) and thought, "Yes, I am going to get Blake…and I AM going by myself."

I drove, I cried, I drove, I cried for the next four hours. I found my way to the Walmart parking lot and there near a cubby hole in the garden section sat Blake, surrounded by his six garbage bags. I knew as soon as I looked into his eyes that I wasn't talking to my son. He got in the car and said he was using, and that he was going to use when he got back home, and there was nothing or no one who was going to stop him. He kept looking at his arms where he had stuck the needles. He was hiding nothing from me.

I felt like a time bomb was ticking. I had fewer than four hours in the car to say something that would change his mind… change his life; to convince my son that his life was worth living. The way he looked at me when he exclaimed, "I don't care if I live or die, mom," went right through me. I believe he meant it.

I told him, "If you make the decision to use, you cannot come back to the house." He had an apartment, and I told him I would take him there. I remember the most heart-wrenching feeling when I dropped him off at the place where he was kidnapped. He didn't want to go back there. The memories of that experience were horrendous.

I asked him not to call me, not to see me until he had decided differently about his choices. I watched him walk away from the car and out of sight. I don't know how I drove the rest of the way home that night. I sobbed so hard, I could hardly see the road.

I spent another week in bed in a fetal position. Most people thought I was still recovering from my appendectomy, but I was trying to mend my broken heart.

After a few weeks, Blake called and said, "Mom? I have done a lot of thinking. I don't want to live my life like this anymore. I miss my son. I miss my family, and I want to live. Can I please come home?" I set strong boundaries: should you decide to use, you must immediately leave the house and your belongings will be on the front porch.

That fall, I believe a miracle happened. It was as if my prayers were answered. Treatment strategies began to cement and relationships began to heal. Days added up to weeks, months, and years where "using" had ceased.

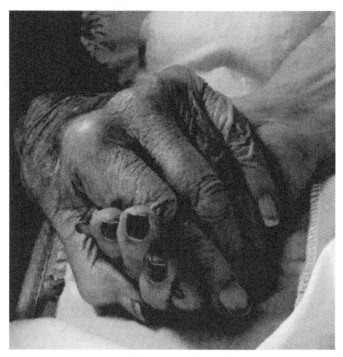

My parents' hands
May 7, 2016

18. Coming Full Circle

As I sat in an indoor pool chair at a state park lodge on a cold day in March 2012, I pondered the concept of "full circle" at that point in our family's journey. I couldn't help but smile watching my two grandsons, Brady and Tyler, horseplay in the pool. That's what boys do. I remembered watching my sons in the pool enjoying themselves the same way.

The pool was filled with children's laughter and screams, their squeaky voices yelling for moms and dads to watch their jumps into the water. Weekends like that reminded me of the wonderful times I spent with my sons. It also brought up memories of being a little girl and playing in the pool with my sisters. Fifty years ago, my parents were smiling at us.

My parents...

Like so many timelines in this circle of life, one is never prepared for inevitable events like watching your parents grow old. In my heart, my parents remain young, vibrant, dependable, and fully accountable. There is the happy memory of dinner time with my parents, grandpa, and four little girls around the table eating the best home cooked meal while talking, giggling, and spilling milk. At that time, I never envisioned life being any different for my parents, but in their eighties, it certainly is. Their forgetfulness and feebleness is heart wrenching.

All my years growing up, my parents protected me. Now it appears roles have reversed, and I am trying to protect them. They will not budge from the four-story home where we all shared our laughter and tears. Anyone who has walked this path knows there is a fine line to cross in deciding to tell your parents what is best for them.

My dad has always been my hero. He supported his family driving an eighteen-wheeler all of his life. How can I tell him it may be unsafe for him to drive his car? "Take away my keys, take away my life," he told me. My mom made the best dinners. Now, she finds it difficult to recall her favorite recipe. She does not cook any more. We miss her dinners immensely.

Life does come full circle for all of us who are blessed with long lives. God has a plan, the future becomes the present, and all we can do is the best we can do. "It is what it is," as the saying goes.

In recent years, my sister and I have made regular trips to Arizona to visit our biological mother, Theresa, especially since her husband's death. Cassie and I have assumed the responsibilities of maintaining good care for her in the Alzheimer's care facility where she now resides. By necessity, we drop everything at home and visit her every other month to coordinate appointments with her medical and financial people. This last visit, as I was hugging her and saying goodbye, she looked me straight in the eyes and said, "I am proud of you." I don't think her present cognitive abilities allowed her to see my tears flowing or the meaning behind them. I have been able to put the past in the past and reaffirm to myself that my mother did the best she could; maybe that's all she had to give. I have inherited several positive qualities from her, and for those I am appreciative. Last year in a Mother's day card I wrote the words, "Thanks for giving me life."

It has been twenty-six years since my marriage to Taylor ended. I can say from my heart that I continue to care for his well-being. He is the father of my sons. I wish only good things for him. The wonder of it all is that we are friends and are there for each other. We share holidays, celebrations, and the birthdays of our children and grandchildren. That is a gift.

Mike thinks his place in my affection is behind Blake's addiction. That notion couldn't be further from the truth. From the very first time I held him in my arms, he had my heart. Some of my best years were spent watching Mike grow up. As an adult, he has been my rock. He is wise beyond his years and experience. Through it all, his genuine goodness has remained constant. Mike works hard to support his family and live the dream. He has several years of abstinence behind him and believes, in his words, "There's no looking or going back."

Mike and his wife, Dana are celebrating their tenth wedding anniversary. While there are the ups and downs of everyday life, living paycheck to paycheck, they remain faithful, loyal, and supportive of each other. They have brought into this world three more grandchildren who are my loves and a source of joy.

When I spend time with my grandchildren, time stands still. All I hear is their laughter. That's all that matters.

I am blessed to have a wonderful relationship with my teenage grandson, Brady. He holds a special place in my heart as my first grandchild. Every Thursday morning at 7:00 am, we keep a date to share donuts before I take him to school. It was his idea! I also cherish our conversations about roller coasters, sports, and now girls. Sometimes we watch football games while munching on his favorite pizza. Thank God that we never walked away and we never gave up hope.

This is where I was four years ago, and I am happy to say that my family has continued on a positive, loving path.

19. A Donor Recipient's Story in Honor of Casey

As a family, each year on April 12, we come together to commemorate Casey's leaving this world. We go to the cemetery and write our messages to him on helium balloons. After a prayer and a few words from Casey's dad, we simultaneously release our balloon messages to the sky to reach him in heaven.

This past April 12, my sister, Casey's mother, received a package in the mail. It was a special candle with this message inside:

I want to share this candle with you. It is a replica of the candle I light every 12th day of April. It is in celebration of my second chance in life, and in deepest gratitude for your son's gift in 2002. Here is my story:

When I was nine years old, I developed Type 1 diabetes. I dealt with the condition all of my life and began experiencing kidney problems in my 20's. After becoming pregnant in 1995, my kidneys failed.

I always felt tired and my lack of energy became a way of life—I started to think that it was my new normal. Each morning I would wake up, sit in bed and think, I have this whole day ahead of me. I had to push myself to meet my responsibilities and struggled to keep up with my young son. When he got a new bike and was nagging me to go riding, I had to sit and watch.

In the fall of 2001, I was listed for a kidney and pancreas transplant. I was ready for a long wait, as doctors predicted it could be years before a transplant came. My family supported me, especially my husband's grandfather, Papa. He always called me his little girl and stayed positive rooting for me to get my transplant.

On April 12, 2002, Papa passed away and my family was devastated. Since I was waiting for a transplant when he died, my husband's family asked us not to attend the funeral, encouraging us to stay home in case we got 'the call.' We thought there was a slim chance I would get a call so quickly, but we reluctantly stayed home.

We were shocked when we received news the next day that a kidney and pancreas had become available for me. We joke that Papa made it happen, that as soon as he got to heaven he found a match for me! I do know he was looking down on me, smiling, knowing that my life would go on because of this amazing gift.

Immediately following my surgery, I felt better than I had in years, and I was ready to go!

I am so thankful for this second chance. I am here for the little things, the everyday things, and *the opportunity to have one more day...and another after that.*

At the end of the day, I am grateful for the fact that I am here, and I am able to just BE. I am able to share smiles, hugs, kisses, kind words, and lend a helping hand when needed. The 'little' things that, when you look back and reflect on life, are really the big things, because these are the moments that bring us joy—

Thanks to my donor that 12th day of April, 2002.
- D. R.

20. A Different Intervention

In February 2013 I headed to Chicago with Blake. He asked me to join him for the six-hour ride to his next intervention. I am really looking forward to spending some one-on-one time with my son. It has been a long time. We talked and laughed on the way. We talked about childhood memories, the good ones.

The time flew quickly, and we had reached our destination. The families usually make the hotel arrangements since they are familiar with the surroundings. The GPS took us to a rundown place that reminded us of a no-tell motel. Blake and I looked at each other, and he assured me, "Don't worry mom, there's a BMW in the parking lot." Oh, that made me feel a lot better. We put a key into a second story outside door and walked in.

There was only one double-size bed in the room. I immediately pulled back the sheets and looked for bed creatures. There was no TV remote, no bath towels, and no toilet seat cover. All I could do was laugh, but Blake did not see the humor at all. He offered to get another room for me. In this motel? By myself? I don't think so!

When I awoke the next morning, I was nervous in anticipation of observing this intervention for a twenty-two-year-old son. My stomach was rolling. We drove to a nearby restaurant to meet the parents of Anthony. Shortly after that, ten more family members joined us. Blake began to orchestrate the intervention. He asked non-directive questions to each family member to uncover the dynamics of the relationships with Anthony. The family spoke of special memories with Anthony.

I could hardly believe what was happening in front of me. Blake was so confident and dedicated to this family. I caught myself looking at him and thinking this is my son! Blake had a plan, and this family to whom he was a total stranger just the day before, was hanging onto his every word. The process was methodical; Blake knew what he was doing, and he was doing it well.

The day before, Blake had instructed the family members to write heartfelt letters to Anthony. Blake collected them and excused himself to go to his car and read them. The letters revealed to Blake who had the most influence with Anthony. When he returned, he asked the father about the physical layout of the living room in their home. I did not understand the reasoning until I saw the home.

Blake asked each one of them if they had any more questions and if they were ready to do this. They were ready…and so was Blake. When we arrived at the home where Anthony lived, Blake directed each person to an assigned seat in the living room. He asked Anthony's older brother, David, to go upstairs and ask Anthony to come down.

When Anthony entered the room, Blake introduced himself and immediately began the process. The order in which they would speak was already planned. I watched Blake as he inconspicuously observed Anthony's body language while the family members were reading their letters. Blake seemed so in tune with the dynamics of this family.

Anthony became fidgety. Blake asked him if he wanted to take a breather. He did, and his brother David accompanied him into another room, as Blake had pre-arranged. Then all hell broke loose. We heard yelling and cursing and felt walls shaking. David and Anthony were going at it. I looked at Blake, with fear in my eyes, but Blake remained calm. After what seemed like a lifetime, Blake entered the room with the brothers and everything grew quiet. A few minutes later, Blake emerged and told the family members anxiously waiting on the other side of the door, "He's going." How did he do that? What just happened?

In less than twenty minutes, the family was hugging Anthony goodbye. Blake had already placed Anthony's bags in the car. While Blake gave the family time say their goodbyes, he knew time was of the essence. Anthony or any of the family members could change their minds. Within minutes, we were heading to another state for Anthony's recovery from this terrible disease.

After a three-hour car ride, we arrived at the door of the treatment center. I stepped out of the car and looked into Anthony's eyes, and said, "Make it work, Anthony. You are a great young man. Never give up hope." I saw a little boy's scared eyes in this young man. His lip was quivering and when we hugged, I felt his chest trembling.

When Blake walked Anthony through the same front doors that he had traversed for his treatment, I was overwhelmed with emotion. Re-living Blake's intervention for his addiction, seeing the treatment center again, and spending the day with Anthony and his family was just too much for one day. But I will never forget it.

21. The Ending

As I write this in March 2016, for the moment, this moment, all is well. There is so much to be grateful for. We have many blessings. Every day, I take the opportunity to thank God and Mother Mary for their guidance and never-ending support. I do not take for granted the sobriety of my two sons, not for one single day. I pray for their recovery daily, and thank God for the wonderful miracles He created.

Both of my sons are alive, well, and following their dreams. Blake is now married to the girl of his dreams. Both of my "daughters-in-love" hold a special place in my heart. My grandchildren are so very precious.

I can only hope that this disease of addiction stops at this generation. I pray that my grandchildren and their children do not live under the suffocating, devastating effects of this disease.

Blake continues as an interventionist. He has traveled across the country helping other families understand the deadly grasp of addiction. Blake notes, "It's the moms that break my heart. I see how their lives are consumed trying to protect their son or daughter while they are enabling them to use." My mind flashes back to Blake as a little guy wanting to take home that dirt bike.

And now, he is travelling across the United States as an interventionist, helping others with their addictions.

Blake has accompanied many kindred hearts of gold to rehab centers to begin a new life and another chance to live, and many of them are doing just that to this day.

Blake rarely shares his intervention experiences. At times, the only information I have is the state he is flying to. But when he calls me, I can hear in his voice the severity of his client's opposition to getting help. He puts so much energy, motivation, and heart into the intervention process. It's in his voice, many miles away.

It amazes me how families welcome Blake into their homes. Prior to the intervention, the family speaks to Blake several times over the phone. Once he arrives in their city, they welcome Blake into their homes and their hearts.

Recently, Blake shared with me a heart-wrenching experience during an intervention with a family's young son. The night before the intervention, Blake met with the family and discussed the concept of "enabling." Everyone was on board and anxiously awaiting the next morning.

The parents, an aunt, brothers, and sisters gathered early that day. When the son arrived, he quickly put together what was happening and immediately grew angry and defiant. No amount of reasoning, discussion, or reading from a bottom-line letter lessened his anger. Alan was leaving. He was out of there. He got in his car, but his father stood in front of it in an attempt to block him. The father was confronting the disease. Alan screamed at his dad to get out of the way, but he did not budge. Alan threatened to call the police. The threat became real. When the police arrived, they told the parent he was obstructing. The dad said, "I am standing in the way of my son's addiction and trying to save his life." The policeman said, "Sir, you either move away from the car, or we will have to handcuff you." The dad remained strong. He wasn't going to passively watch from the sidelines while this disease was killing his son.

The police officers handcuffed the dad and escorted him to the cruiser. Alan's face, lacking any emotion, watched as his tearful father was handcuffed and placed in the cruiser. When the cruiser drove out of sight, Blake turned to Alan and said, "We are done here."

Within a few hours, the father was released. He called Blake and said, "Let's try again, I am not giving up; there is always hope." They searched for Alan the rest of the day without luck. Alan returned home the next morning on his own and told his father, "I am ready, dad, let's call that interventionist." Within the next few hours, Blake was accompanying Alan to rehab. Thank God.

If we had lost Blake to this disease in that God-awful hotel room, there would most likely be another interventionist to take his place throughout these years. But maybe, just maybe, it was Blake who reached that one addict who decided to get help and seek recovery. And just maybe, it was that one person whose life was saved by God and rehab through Blake.

I often wonder why and how we got through the perils of

addiction. There were times when I really was not certain we all would survive. I sometimes questioned how God could let this happen in our family. There is no discrimination when it comes to addiction. If there was an answer to the question, "Why," it might be in the following testimonial to Blake from a parent following an intervention:

It is so hard to know what to do during these emotionally charged times. We have swung from angry, sad, confused and even trying to figure out what we could have done differently. Blake has helped us see that all of the emotions that we are going through are normal and that we are not alone going down the path of having a son who needs help, and thankfully with the help of Blake, is now in a place to get help. This is a road, that as a parent, you never really think you will be going down, these things seem to happen to others but in reality they happen to all different kinds of people no matter where you are from or what kind of life you have tried to give your children or the opportunities that exist for them. Blake has been a pillar of strength, knowledge, experience, and kindness that has given our family someone to trust and help guide us through this time. Without Blake, our son would not be getting the help he needs and without a doubt we would not be on the positive path and not have the hope and the belief that we have done all we could to get him there. There are few times in life when you meet someone who truly touches your life and this is one of them. Thank you, Blake, for all your kindness. Your mother must be very proud to have you as her son.

There is always hope. I believe that with all my heart. Hope is what got me here today. There were days when there was little hope…there were times when hope was all that was left.

Today, I received a letter from a young lady who is desperately trying to be free from her drug addiction. She writes:

Dear Pam,

I just wanted to tell you how thankful and blessed I am to have you in my life. Thank you for never giving up on me. I never want to waste an opportunity to tell someone who has impacted my life as much as you have that I appreciate and love them. I read a quote I liked and can relate to. 'Never deprive someone of hope; it might be all they have.'

22. Message from a Mother's Heart

I believe two of the greatest miracles in my life are the births of my sons. I had no idea I could love someone as much as I love them. They have been my life. Right or wrong, that is the way it has been. I know I over-protected them as they were growing up. I know I was their biggest enabler through their addictions.

I trusted them and all their spoken words. Why would they lie to their mother? How could they lie to me? While writing the words of this book, it was heartbreaking to relive some of these experiences. It reminded me how devastated and scared I felt. I was fearful to think I could lose my sons to this dreadful disease.

There were times I became so absorbed in trying to "fix" their lives that I almost lost mine. There were times I was surrounded by the support of my extended family. There were times I stood alone.

I would cry, then cry some more. There were times I was numb and unable to cry or laugh.

During those times, I turned to my higher power. I truly believe He gave me the strength to be hopeful. I believe that prayer is what saved my sons. And prayer continues to work for their sobriety today.

I am grateful that I was able to continue to have hope. At times the ray of hope appeared to be a small flicker of light, but it never went out in my heart. My son, Blake told me recently, "Mom, you never gave up hope for me, and for that I am so grateful."

Both of my sons have hearts full of hope. And so does this mom. There is always hope.

.

Blake Today

Recovery Help

My whole life, both personally and professionally, has been dedicated to helping others. Coping with my sons' addictions has taught me the difference between helping and enabling. There is always hope.
I can be reached at pbasil09@gmail.com

This book honors the memory of the woman
I called "mom" all my life.
She went to heaven on May 7, 2016.

Thank you for reading my book. If you enjoyed it, please take a moment to leave me a review at the book retailer.

Made in the USA
Columbia, SC
31 October 2023